Contents

ON THE MOVE 4

PLANNING YOUR TRIP 6

GETTING THERE 12

WHERE TO STAY 20

BRIGHT LIGHTS, BIG CITY 26

HEALTH AND SAFETY 32

TROUBLESHOOTING 40

THINK GREEN 48

QUIZ RESULTS 50

20 THINGS TO REMEMBER 51

FURTHER INFORMATION 52

GLOSSARY 54

INDEX 56

Some words are printed in bold, **like this**. You can find out
what they mean by looking in the glossary.

On The Move

Right now, millions of people are on the move, travelling about the planet. People today travel more than ever before. Whether for business or pleasure, we travel further in a year than most of our ancestors travelled in a lifetime. Technology and cheap fares mean many of us are able to travel to other countries easily and speedily. Never before has travel been such big business.

DID YOU KNOW?

The average person spends one hour and six minutes travelling every day. In a year, each person travels an average of 12,000 km (7,400 miles). Everyone on the planet in total travels almost 25 trillion km (17 trillion miles) in a year. Of all this travelling:

- 53 percent is by car;
- 26 percent is by bus;
- 9 percent is by rail;
- 9 percent is by high-speed transport, such as planes;
- 3 percent is by bicycle, boat, and other means.

A LONG HAUL

People take approximately 800 million journeys to foreign countries each year, a number that is expected to double by 2020. Where do all these international travellers go? Most go to France. After that, Spain and the United States are top choices, followed by China and Italy. Almost a third go to the United Kingdom.

The most popular destinations for young travellers are Australia, the United States, and France. Back-packers often head for Thailand, Australia, and New Zealand. Three out of four young travellers travel to explore, learn a language, do volunteer-work, or study. Four out of five say they return more tolerant of other cultures as a result of their travels.

"The world is a book and those who do not travel read only a page."
Saint Augustine, Philosopher

TRAVEL TIPS

John Townsend

Heinemann
LIBRARY

| | www.heinemannlibrary.co.uk | **To order:** |
Visit our website to find out more information about Heinemann Library books.

To order:
☎ Phone +44 (0) 1865 888066
🖷 Fax +44 (0) 1865 314091
🖳 Visit www.heinemannlibrary.co.uk

Heinemann Library is an imprint of Capstone Global Library Limited, a company incorporated in England and Wales having its registered office at 7 Pilgrim Street, London, EC4V 6LB – Registered company number: 6695582

Heinemann is a registered trademark of Pearson Education Limited, under licence to Capstone Global Library Limited

Text © Capstone Global Library Limited 2009
First published in hardback in 2009
Paperback edition first published in 2010

Edited by Pollyanna Poulter
Designed by Philippa Jenkins and Hart MacLeod
Original illustrations © Pearson Education Limited by Clare Elsom
Picture research by Elizabeth Alexander and Maria Joannou
Production by Alison Parsons
Originated by Modern Age Repro House Ltd
Printed and bound in China by South China Printing Company Ltd

ISBN 978 0 431112 38 1 (hardback)
13 12 11 10 09
10 9 8 7 6 5 4 3 2 1

ISBN 978 0 431112 54 1 (paperback)
14 13 12 11 10
10 9 8 7 6 5 4 3 2 1

British Library Cataloguing-in-Publication Data
Townsend, John, 1955-
Travel tips. - (Life skills)
910.2
A full catalogue record for this book is available from the British Library.

Acknowledgements
We would like to thank the following for permission to reproduce photographs: © Alamy Images: pp. 5 (David Noble Photography), **13** (ImageState), **33** (JLImages), **45** (Charles Ridgway), **46** (Terry Sohl); © Corbis: pp. **7**, **25** (Moodboard), **29** (Jose Fuste Raga), **37** (Tom Bean); © Getty Images: pp. **18** (Taxi/Carlos Spottorno), **43** (Photographer's Choice/Fredrik Skold), **49** (AFP Photo/Eric Cabanis); © Lonely Planet Images: p. **38** (Andrew Marshall & Leanne Walker); © Masterfile: p. **31** (Noel Hendrickson); © Photolibrary: pp. **8** (Christie & Cole), **21** (Duncan McDougall); © Public Health Image Library: p. **35** (James Gathany); © Rex Features: pp. **15** (Sipa Press), **17**; © Science Photo Library: p. **11** (BSIP, LA); © Still Pictures: pp. **23** (Vélez/Andia), **27** (Nigel Dickinson).

Cover photograph of tourist taking picture reproduced with permission of © Istockphoto (Sharon Dominick).

We would like to thank Helena Smith for her invaluable help in the preparation of this book.

Every effort has been made to contact copyright holders of material reproduced in this book. Any omissions will be rectified in subsequent printings if notice is given to the Publishers.

By 2020, 378 million **long-haul** travellers will be on the move each year, many of them young people. Whether visiting new places with school, college, family, or friends, young travellers can learn about the world through real, unforgettable experiences.

One day you, too, may join friends on a "gap year" and set off to explore new areas. Wherever you plan to go, you want to get the most from life's journeys, no matter where they take you. That's where this book can help!

The world's top tourist destinations, 2006	
Country	**Millions of visitors**
1. France	79.1
2. Spain	58.5
3. United States	51.1
4. China	49.6
5. Italy	41.1
6. United Kingdom	30.7
7. Germany	23.6
8. Mexico	21.4
9. Austria	20.3
10. Russian Federation	20.2

Even if you haven't been to another country, it's still likely that you'll take at least a few trips abroad in your lifetime.

PLANNING YOUR TRIP

So you've saved up and it's almost time for "the off". Before you walk out the door and wave goodbye, there are a few things to make sure of – wherever you're going. After all, time spent planning can save hours of misery while you're away.

LOOK AHEAD

Of the billions of trips every year, the majority go perfectly well and travellers return home looking forward to their next journey. But holidays or travelling can go badly wrong, for all sorts of reasons. Poor planning before even setting off is one of those reasons. It always pays to plan ahead.

> "No one realizes how beautiful it is to travel until he comes home and rests his head on his old, familiar pillow."
> Lin Yutang, Chinese writer

Do your research

It's always a good idea to find out some key facts about a destination. Apart from giving ideas of extra places to go, research might suggest times to avoid. After all, it's not a good idea to arrive somewhere in the grip of a **hurricane**, transport strike, epidemic, political unrest, or traffic gridlock. Research is also a good way to spark up the travel mood.

Getting it Right

Before you start planning, ask:

- **Where?** City or countryside? Hot or cold? Coast or inland? Culture or action? Many people head to the same places. For example, many Britons head for Spain, France, Greece, or Florida.

- **When?** When is the best time to travel? It pays to consider weather, times of the year, transport timetables, and when attractions open or close for the season.

- **Why?** After an adventure? Visiting friends or family? On a school-exchange? There are many good reasons for travelling. Knowing what yours are will help you enjoy your trip even more!

A few searches on the Internet might reveal all kinds of interesting information that could improve a visit. You could also go to your local library and browse the travel section for any useful books.

Be prepared

Young people who aren't used to travelling can sometimes feel **homesick** when they're away. But young people aren't the only ones who miss family, friends, pets, and familiar things. It's quite normal for all people to miss home. Some people may only feel slight loneliness, sadness, or anxiety. Others may develop stomachache or headache. Usually when the new surroundings become more familiar, feelings of homesickness go away.

To deal with homesickness:

- Pack photos, letters, or a favourite object to keep a bit of home close to hand.

- Talk to others. A problem shared is often a problem halved.

- Write feelings down on paper if there is no one to talk to.

- Keep in touch with people at home by texting or sending an email (just remember to include such costs in your travel budget).

WHAT TO PACK

"Just in case" can be bad advice when packing for a trip! Most people are tempted to cram everything in "just in case". What to pack and what to leave behind is worth thinking about long before it's time to depart.

Some people leave packing to the last minute and don't think about the essential things they will need. Other travellers start making long lists of what to pack months before they go.

The number-one rule when packing is "if in doubt, leave it out". Moving heavy bags on and off trains, buses, and crowded stairways can be bad news – for everyone. Besides, the more you take, the more there is to lose.

Wherever possible, keep to one bag only. When hiking, just one rucksack is the limit. Always remember, even cases with wheels can be awkward to move through busy streets or rough countryside, especially in bad weather.

Although people have different requirements, there are some basic things everyone needs on their travels. Depending on the destination, many items can be bought cheaply in most supermarkets around the world, so if they get left behind, it's not a big deal.

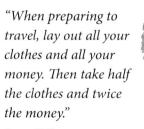

"When preparing to travel, lay out all your clothes and all your money. Then take half the clothes and twice the money."

Susan Heller,
American writer

Trying to pack too much is a common problem!

• CHECKLIST •

- Everyday bag: to keep items you often use handy (tickets, camera, reading material).

- First aid kit: compact travel health kit, small nail scissors, and tweezers.

- Toiletries (in a waterproof bag): toothpaste; toothbrush; hairbrush or comb; shampoo; soap; mini towel or sarong; deodorant, etc.

- Mobile phone and charger (and adapter if you are going abroad).

- Money carrier and small padlock. Use a money belt or neck wallet to keep money (and passport when abroad) secure.

- Travel watch or alarm.

- Torch or head lamp.

- Sunglasses and sun cream: protect your eyes and skin from harmful rays, especially if travelling at higher altitudes, in bright sunlight, or in snow.

- Travel organiser: for carrying identification, tickets, addresses, and phone numbers.

- Positive attitude! Travel sometimes means dealing with the unexpected, so it always helps to take along a big smile.

Getting it Right

Cramming the most stuff into a small bag is a skill. Remember to put the items that will be needed first on arrival at the top. Plenty of plastic bags are helpful, too. Some travellers prefer to roll up clothes for packing, to reduce creases. Small, soft items, such as socks, are good for packing round hard edges or anything breakable. Remember to pack small items inside shoes to save space, and don't forget to label luggage clearly.

GOING ABROAD

It was once rare for young people to visit other countries. Today, international travel is common for millions of young travellers. The first time abroad can be both exciting and daunting, particularly if the traveller doesn't speak the language. This is why it pays to learn as much as you can about a country and its customs, rules, and **etiquette** before you travel to it.

How passports work

A passport is an internationally recognised travel document that proves the identity and nationality of the traveller. A current passport is required to enter and leave most countries.

A **visa** is a special document that may be required to enter another country, especially for travellers who plan to work in that country or stay for a long period. A visa must be obtained from the embassy of the country you are visiting. Details and advice can be obtained from the Passport Office.

In some countries, you must carry your passport at all times. If not, it's always best to leave the passport somewhere safe, making sure there's a photocopy somewhere else. Should the passport get lost or stolen, the copy should help the nearest **embassy** get a replacement within a few days.

Getting it Right

When entering and leaving countries, it is necessary to go through customs, where travellers and their luggage may be searched. Make sure you are not carrying anything forbidden or anyone else's luggage.

Other preparations

Before travelling to other countries, first find out which **vaccinations** are required. The World Health Organisation provides up-to-date information on which inoculations are needed for different countries. It clearly states: *"It is the traveller's responsibility to ask for information, to understand the risks involved, and to take the necessary precautions for the journey."*

Foreign money is often confusing so it's well worth doing some homework to find out the exact **exchange rate**. A good online currency converter can show the value of most world currencies. It's just a matter of typing in an amount of money and clicking a button to get its value in another currency. Easy!

People in different countries do not all set their clocks and watches to show the same time as yours. Instead, people live in different time zones. Check what time zone you are travelling to, and be prepared to change your watch to the local time.

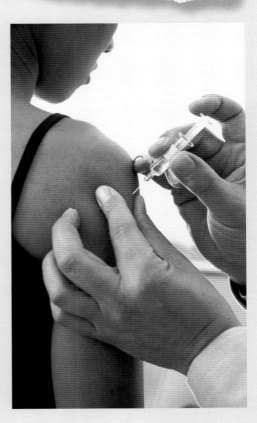

For security, take some money in the form of traveller's cheques. Or keep your money in an account at home and use ATMs to withdraw it.

Visit your doctor at least a month in advance of your trip, to find out which inoculations you will need.

GETTING THERE

You've done your research, packed your bags, and you're ready to go – but the big question facing every traveller is, "How?" What type of transport is best? The answer to that question very much depends on where you hope to go.

MANY ROADS TO CROSS

Wherever you plan to travel, whether near home or far away, you're actually more likely to use roads than anything else. In fact, 80 percent of all travel is by road. While there are more roads in the United States than anywhere else, Europe's roads are far busier.

Bicycle

Many young people get their first taste of independent travel from setting off by bike to explore areas close to home before venturing further. Some adventurous travellers put their bike on a bus or train then explore a new area by pedal power on the open road. Bicycle hire or **tandem** hire with a friend (it has to be a *good* friend!) is a great way to see new places.

DID YOU KNOW?

The world's worst traffic jam happened in France in the summer of 2001. The queue stretched 660 km (410 miles), from Paris to Toulouse.

TIP

For long bicycle journeys:

- Relax as you ride, and take a break every hour;
- Eat frequently, in small amounts;
- Stay well hydrated;
- Avoid numb hands by wearing cycling gloves;
- Take talcum powder to avoid and treat chafing;
- Plan for all weathers (for details about checking weather conditions see page 52).

Car travel

Most families tend to travel for at least part of their holiday by car. Cramming in luggage, the dog, food, and other extras can be a nightmare! As can a long journey if the travellers feel bored, sick, or both!

You can prevent carsickness by being prepared. Always bring games or activities to do if you go on a long car journey. Sitting in the front of the car, or having a clear view of the road, also helps. Singing along to music, or playing games that encourage looking ahead, can prevent problems. And make sure the car is well ventilated.

Buses

One of the best ways for young people to travel cheaply is by bus, so it's always worth considering the services available. (See page 52 for more information on national bus services.)

Getting it Right

Moving from one place to another has always carried risks. Roads can be dangerous things – particularly in unfamiliar places. Whether you plan to cycle or just walk, you need to be aware of the "rules of the road" wherever you happen to be. An important rule for young people travelling by road is never hitchhike, not even in a group.

When travelling around the United States, Canada, or Australia, the famous Greyhound buses have routes to and from thousands of places.

BOATS AND TRAINS

Sea travel has always held great excitement, mystery, and adventure. Sadly, it can also hold storms, icebergs, and seasickness! Even so, going on cruise ships has never been more popular. Cruises designed especially for young people are more and more common.

With some cruises, travellers can step on or off ships at any port along their journey. Without all the extras of large, expensive cruises, some options allow student travellers to get across the seas much more cheaply. But remember: the smaller the ship, the greater the chance of feeling seasick.

Rail travel

If sailing the oceans doesn't appeal, how about a glamorous train journey across Russia and China along the famous Silk Route? The Trans-Siberian Express and China Orient Express are among the world's most **prestigious** trains.

Travelling by train can be a great way to get around and see the world through a window, often with the most spectacular scenery. Some young people may dismiss rail travel as being too expensive, but it doesn't have to be.

Getting it Right

To ease seasickness:

- Get as much fresh air as possible away from the smell of fuel fumes and food. Go out on deck and focus on the horizon or something that isn't moving – don't watch the waves!

- Inside, find a seat in the middle of the ship on a lower deck. This is where the ship moves least.

- Avoid heavy meals before travelling.

- Lie still with your eyes shut.

- Anti-sickness medicines should be taken before travel, and according to the instructions, so they have time to be absorbed by the body.

- Ginger biscuits help some people, or ginger tea. Also pack some peppermint sweets or tea, as both can help with seasickness.

- **Acupressure** can be applied with a wristband or by pressing a finger against the middle of the wrist.

Look out for special deals or passes for young travellers, and keep in mind some of the points in favour of rail travel.

- Trains allow travellers to move easily between cities. Most train stations are near tourist centres and have hotels nearby.

- Sleeping on sleeper trains saves time and some of the cost of a hotel.

- Moving effortlessly between destinations on a train, travellers can talk to local passengers, get travel information from other travellers, read a good book, or just sit back and enjoy the view!

- It's a greener way to travel than by bus or plane.

Maybe not all trains let you relax – you might not always get a seat!

UP AND AWAY

The average number of travellers flying over the United States in any hour is about 61,000 people. That equals millions of air passengers in a whole year! Of them, approximately five million are people younger than 18, travelling alone. In fact, air travel for young people is big business, and they are well looked after by many airlines!

DID YOU KNOW?

People who are younger than 15 and who travel alone are usually called "unaccompanied minors" by airlines. Different airlines have different rules and services for unaccompanied minors, so the advice is: always contact the airline well in advance of a booking to find out the procedure.

Check before flying

The rules about how much luggage you can take on planes are forever changing, so it's important to check with the airline before you pack. What is banned to carry in hand luggage can also change from airport to airport and in other countries, so it pays to check in advance to avoid substances or items being confiscated. Also, don't forget that luggage can get lost, so never pack valuables!

When you are ready to go to the airport, always set off with plenty of time to spare. Check traffic reports for any likely delays. Many people fail to give themselves enough time to get to the airport. Minimum check-in times vary. The latest cut-off is usually 30 minutes before the departure time, but for long-haul flights check-in is often much earlier.

When checking in for your flight, be sure to confirm any special requests, such as meal specifications, that you made when booking your flight. If you suffer from airsickness, ask for a seat over the wing, where the plane is most stable. Tilt your seat back, rest your head on the headrest, and close your eyes.

Listening to music helps some people relax and can take their mind off feeling unwell or frightened of flying. However, you must switch off electrical equipment during take-off and landing, as they can interfere with the aircraft's computer signals.

Bad weather or mechanical problems can destroy the best planning – but you should get there eventually!

When things go wrong

In an ideal world, airlines would never have delays, no flights would be cancelled, and the weather would stay fine. But in the real world, even with the best-laid plans, weather can turn nasty and connections can be missed. When flights don't run to plan, always stay calm and be patient.

If your flight is cancelled, remain at the gate with other passengers and listen for instructions. There may be free meal certificates or hotel vouchers being given out. Ask at your airline's desk about re-booking a flight that has been cancelled.

Getting it Right

- Never try to hide anything at the airport.

- Keep a note of your flight number handy, as well as the time of departure and the terminal from which you are departing.

- Keep a good reading book handy in case of long waits at the airport.

During the flight

Pay close attention to the safety talk at the beginning of the flight so you know where to find your nearest exit and what to do in case of an emergency. Keep yourself feeling good on the flight by drinking juice or water, to ensure you are hydrated. Try doing seated leg exercises to help prevent stiffness.

On arrival

On arrival at your destination, report any problems (such as damaged or lost baggage) to the airline before leaving the airport. If damage was impossible to notice until much later, call the airline as soon as possible to find out what to do.

Getting it Wrong

- Never joke about hijackings or bombings. It is against the law.
- Never accept parcels or letters from strangers, and never carry anything onto a plane for anyone else.
- Never leave your luggage unattended.

Despite some people being worried about flying, it can be relaxing and is one of the safest ways to travel.

QUIZ

GETTING THERE

1) When planning to travel, what is most important?
a) Going to a quiet place far from other people.
b) Getting a real bargain with lots of cheap attractions.
c) Finding a tourist centre that's great fun with lots to do and plenty to buy.

2) When packing your bags, what do you take?
a) As few clothes as possible, as personal hygiene doesn't matter when you're away.
b) As much as you can so you don't have to buy anything when you're away.
c) All your best clothes so you're ready to party.

3) When planning a trip, do you:
a) get a book from the library about remote wilderness holidays?
b) search the Internet for budget fares and economy accommodation?
c) ask a travel agent to do the lot for you and let them choose?

4) To get to your destination, do you:
a) pay a bit extra to make sure you don't have to sit with young children and tourists?
b) get the cheapest ticket even if it means sleeping at the station between connections?
c) choose the fastest and most exciting way to travel?

5) What is your idea of a perfect meal when travelling?
a) A delicious meal you've cooked for yourself on a campfire under the stars.
b) Getting invited to someone's home to sample the local cooking and company.
c) A candle-lit dinner with lots of people and piles of food cooked by an award-winning chef.

6) Who do you like to be with on your travels most of all?
a) Yourself.
b) Local people who treat you as their guest.
c) Friends you make when travelling.

See page 50 to find out what kind of traveller you are!

WHERE TO STAY

Think about where you want to stay before you try to find accommodation. Some people insist on comfort, style, and luxury while others just want a bed for the night for the lowest price possible. The more you pay, the better the service is likely to be – although that isn't always the case. Horror stories are sometimes told of cockroaches and mice scuttling in expensive accommodation, while some of the cheapest hotels can offer excellent service.

GRADING PLACES

Travel guides and Internet searches are the best way to find out about accommodation. In many countries, hotels are graded with a star system. The more stars the hotel has by its name (often five is the maximum, but not always), the more services it provides. However, there is no international agreement on what the number of stars actually means. It is up to the traveller to check each hotel's list of facilities.

If you do not book accommodation in advance, always view a room before you take it. It is the traveller's right to view a room before committing to stay in it.

(See pages 52 and 53 for details of some useful websites and guides which can assist you with your accommodation planning.)

Getting it Right

It is advisable to book accommodation well in advance, particularly at busy times of the year. When making a reservation by telephone or online, keep a record of a confirmation number, the name of the person who took the reservation, and the quoted rate. Remember that the hotel's tariff, or price, is likely to be higher at the busiest times.

It always pays to check the accommodation before booking, just in case you don't like a railway under your window, bedbugs, dirty bathrooms, bad food, a damp mattress, or dripping ceilings!

TYPES OF ACCOMMODATION

Hotel

A place where guests pay to stay for a short time, sometimes with services such as a restaurant, swimming pool, or meeting rooms. Modern hotels usually have many bedrooms, often with en-suite bathrooms, air-conditioning, and room service. In Australia, a hotel might mean just a pub or a bar.

Guesthouse

Often the name given to a small hotel, offering just a few rooms and limited services to paying guests.

Self-catering accommodation

Where rooms are available to rent. Rooms include a kitchen for travellers to prepare their own meals.

B & B (Bed and Breakfast)

Often a family-run home or farmhouse with a few bedrooms available. Paying guests are given a room to sleep in at night and breakfast the following morning. Guests are expected to leave the premises after breakfast.

Motel

A hotel for motorists. Motels usually have good access to the road network or are purpose-built, out of town, on a major route.

Hostel

Popular with young travellers. Guests can rent a bed, often located in a communal or shared sleeping space. Bathroom, kitchen, and lounge areas are also shared. (See page 22 for more information on hostels.)

YOUTH HOSTELS

An organisation exists for young people on the move that need cheap, reliable accommodation for just a night or two. Today, by joining the Youth Hostel Association (**YHA**), anyone can stay cheaply in one of the thousands of YHA hostels around the world. They provide accommodation where guests can rent a bed (sometimes a bunk bed in a **dormitory**) and share a bathroom, kitchen, and lounge or games room.

One of the great things about staying in a hostel is that you can meet a variety of people, often from many countries. Hostels are places where travellers can share experiences, get to understand other cultures, and make good friendships.

How it started out

Richard Schirrmann was a German schoolteacher. He wanted to enrich the lives of young people living in large cities, by letting them enjoy the countryside. He opened the world's first Youth Hostel in Germany in 1909. The Youth Hostels Association of Great Britain was later formed to combine rambling, cycling, and youth organisations. It provided simple accommodation for walkers and cyclists travelling throughout the United Kingdom.

Finding a hostel

The YHA has 4,000 hostels all around the world in more than 80 countries, under the name Hostelling International (HI). It boasts: "Unlike bland motels, impersonal hotels or dodgy backpacker houses, HI youth hostels are fun, lively meeting places, full of like-minded people." In order to stay at a YHA hostel, be sure to take your YHA membership card with you.

Each year, millions of young people visit the United States from around the world. Hostelling International USA provides travellers with information, a comfortable stay, and access to cheap travel.

The downside of hostel accommodation for some travellers is the lack of privacy. Sharing a dormitory is very different from staying in a private hotel room. There can be noises from people snoring, returning late, or leaving early. That's why many youth hostels fix times for last admissions and lights out.

DID YOU KNOW?

Hostels were once run with very strict rules, where all visitors had to perform cleaning duties and other tasks. Today, they are far more informal. Older people can use hostels, too – so long as they are young at heart!

Getting it
Right

Staying in a hostel can be a good choice because:

- They are low in price compared to hotels and B&Bs;
- Communal areas mean guests mix more than in hotels;
- Most hostels have a good community feel and are far more relaxed than hotels. This gives guests the chance to make new friends and share stories and travel tips;
- Most hostels have a library of travel guides for guests to use to plan their journey;
- Hostel staff are usually friendly and keen to help, providing free advice on local places to check out.

A youth hostel common room is a great place to meet other young travellers.

CAMPING

Walking through the countryside with a backpack is good exercise and a great way to explore nature. There's nothing quite like walking in the great outdoors, pitching a tent, and sleeping under the stars!

Many hikers prefer to use official campsites with all kinds of facilities available. Campsites usually cost just a small amount and provide a safe, clean environment. As for the hiking, the only real cost involved is the equipment needed. With a group of people, a lot can be shared.

Benefits of hiking

- It gives you a chance to get away and forget about the everyday stresses of life.
- It's a way of relaxing but also a chance to test skills and abilities.
- In a hiking party, it's easy to share the various jobs and responsibilities with a group of friends.

It's always better for young or inexperienced hikers to travel in a group. That way, if someone gets hurt or ill, there are others to help. A group of at least three is safest. A lot can be learned from fellow hikers who know more about camping. The best way to learn the basics of camping and to develop skills is to travel with more experienced hikers.

Camping is a healthy way for a group of friends to see new places and enjoy travelling cheaply.

• CHECKLIST •

- Hiking boots and backpack.
- Tent, poles, mallet, ground sheet, sleeping bag, mattress, pillow, blankets, air pump, rope, stakes.
- All-weather clothing (i.e. waterproofs).
- Map, compass, torch and batteries, lantern, drinking water, radio, canteen, clock, camera, tent repair gear, pocket knife, lighter, tissues, water-purification tablets.
- First aid kit with tweezers to remove splinters.
- Kitchen utensils: food container, pans, stove, fuel, matches/lighter, paper plates, bowls, mugs, thermos, aluminium foil, towel, tongs, bottle/can opener, knife, washing-up liquid, sponge, rubbish bags.

Getting it
Right

If staying on a campsite, check the rules and facilities, as there may be all kinds of regulations. If camping "in the wild":

- Make sure you are staying in a place that is not off-limits;

- Find a spot that is safe and protected. Camp away from hilltops, where there's no protection from strong winds and lightning. Avoid the very lowest ground as it might flood in heavy rain;

- Find natural obstacles that provide windbreaks and shelter. Trees and rocks are good natural barriers. Don't pitch a tent right under a tree in case of lightning or falling branches;

- If possible, camp near a stream, river, or lake so there's water for washing and cleaning up. Don't get too close though, in case there are flash floods.

BRIGHT LIGHTS, BIG CITY

Are you dazzled by the bright lights of big cities? Many of us are attracted far more by the hustle and bustle of cities than by camping in the peaceful outdoors. So what do you need to know before visiting a large city that you've never been to before?

CAPITAL COSTS

The first point to bear in mind in the biggest cities of the world is that you often have to pay the biggest prices. The cost of food, entertainment, transport, attractions, and shopping – some of the very reasons many of us like to visit city centres – can be far higher than anywhere else. Although sightseeing in busy, capital cities usually has great appeal, be prepared for huge prices.

Wherever you are in the world, visit local markets and try haggling with the vendors. Fruit, jewellery, clothes, souvenirs ... you name it – you're bound to find some bargains.

TIP

The world's 10 most expensive cities	
City	**Country**
1. Moscow	Russia
2. London	Great Britain
3. Seoul	South Korea
4. Tokyo	Japan
5. Hong Kong	China
6. Copenhagen	Denmark
7. Geneva	Switzerland
8. Osaka	Japan
9. Zurich	Switzerland
10. Oslo	Norway

Mercer's 2007 survey. http://money.cnn com/2007/06/15/pf/most_expensive_cities

According to the cost of transport, food, clothing, housing, household goods, and entertainment, the most expensive city to visit is Moscow, followed by London. Among North American cities, New York and Los Angeles are the most expensive and the only two to rank in the top 50 of the world's most expensive cities.

Despite London being the second most expensive city in the world, more than 15 million travellers from overseas visit Britain's capital every year. Many of them are young students on trips with schools and colleges.

→

Top 10 city destinations 2006		
City	**Ranking**	**Millions of foreign tourist arrivals**
London	1	15.64
Bangkok	2	10.35
Paris	3	9.70
Singapore	4	9.50
Hong Kong	5	8.14
New York City	6	6.22
Dubai	7	6.12
Rome	8	6.03
Seoul	9	4.92
Barcelona	10	4.70

Source: http://www.euromonitor.com/Top_150_City_Destinations_London_Leads_the_Way

Must-see

New York is the top, must-see city in the United States. About 40 million foreign and American tourists visit each year. Among New York's main attractions are the Empire State Building, Ellis Island, Broadway theatre shows, world-class museums, the Bronx Zoo, and New York Botanical Garden. After all that sightseeing, any traveller is likely to be hungry. Here, the choice of places to eat is like nowhere else in the world.

PLANNING AHEAD

When heading for a new city, the temptation is to forget about the homework. After all, cities have everything, so why not wait to get there before worrying about accommodation and places to see? But planning in advance saves travellers a lot of time and expense.

With just a few brochures, guidebooks, a good street plan, and Internet searches, city travellers are ready to take on the whole city experience. Knowing such information in advance helps give a stranger to a city a mental map and idea of where places worth visiting are found in relation to each other.

Getting it Right

Some countries, especially in the Middle East and Asia, dress more conservatively than many Western countries. You shouldn't wear shorts or sleeveless tops in these places. Some holy places, such as St Peter's Cathedral in Rome, Italy, require you to cover your arms when entering the building. You don't want to miss out on seeing such great places just because you don't match the dress code!

DID YOU KNOW?

The World Youth & Student Educational Travel Confederation conducted a worldwide survey of young travellers. The survey shows that 80 percent of young travellers use the Internet to search for travel information before departing, with 50 percent booking transport and accommodation online.

Be street-wise

Wherever you're travelling to, get some local knowledge. Read up on local laws and customs to avoid offending people or breaking local laws without realising it.

Knowing the local street code can prevent visitors being fined or even arrested. For example, just crossing the street in some cities is a **jaywalking** offence, if a proper pedestrian crossing isn't used. Even accidentally dropping a ticket or brochure could be a litter offence, with an instant fine being charged.

Always be aware of belongings and valuables. Be careful when out in crowded streets. Pickpockets are always on the lookout for confused tourists. Be prepared for the worst and leave copies of ticket numbers, your passport, insurance, and contact details somewhere safe – just in case.

Finally, keep with friends, don't wander off alone, and keep your mobile phone handy. Always leave details of your travel plans with someone else, such as family or friends back home. (See page 42 for more on travel and crime.)

Whatever a tourist could wish for, it will be in New York. Maybe that's why so many young people continue to be attracted by the hustle and bustle of this great city.

TIP

Draw up a list of what to see, with a timetable of when to go, having checked opening times, transport links, and closure days.

City travel

Walking around a city might look straightforward on a map and appear easy when first setting off. However, in bad weather, or after a long day of walking around streets, even the hardiest visitor is likely to need another mode of transport. Many cities have excellent transport services around the centres, but the cost of journeys soon mounts up. By checking costs in advance, the city traveller can get some good deals on bus, tram, and train tickets. Often a daily pass is much cheaper than buying tickets for every journey, particularly if many rides are expected.

In some of the larger world capitals, a public transportation service (such as the "tube", a metro, or subway) is a quick way to get around. Get a pocket map of the public transit system in advance, although most stations will have small route maps available. Be warned: maps aren't always to scale. Although stations on the map may look as though they're right next to each other, it probably isn't really the case!

Use common sense when travelling around a city after dark. Stick to main streets, particularly in unfamiliar areas. If you're not sure about a destination or the safety of an area, take a taxi. If you do take the subway or an underground train late at night, ride in cars with more people inside.

DID YOU KNOW?

A British woman recently designed two rings, to be worn on a finger of each hand, that stop the wearer getting lost. With a small control device worn round the neck which displays numbers, the wearer just taps in the post code of a place to find. An electronic compass and GPS system sends signals to the two rings. Small vibrating motors make the rings buzz to tell the wearer to turn left or right, go forwards or backwards. Both rings buzz at once if the person goes in the wrong direction. Maybe we'll all be wearing them soon!

Getting lost

Even with a map, it's quite easy to get lost in some of the bigger cities of the world. Imagine emerging from a Tokyo subway into a huge bustling street and trying to find street signs, without knowing any Japanese. That's why more city travellers are using personal satellite navigation devices (SAT-NAVs) to help them get around. This technology is often called a GPS (Global Positioning Satellite) system.

GPSs can be used in any city in the world. They tell you exactly where you are and how to get to where you want to go.

In the middle of a city, help isn't far away. Just ask for the nearest:

TIP

- Tourist information centre;
- Hospital;
- Embassy (if abroad);
- Police station;
- Reception staff (in a hotel).

Health And Safety

Some people feel that travel is riskier to their health than everyday life. Truth be told, though, the most dangerous part of a trip is the car ride to the airport! In fact, the risk of an inactive lifestyle is greater than travel accidents, natural disasters, and shark attacks all put together.

HARD TO SWALLOW

The majority of travellers have a great and healthy time away. However, there are still precautions every traveller ought to take before setting off, to help avoid the more common health problems.

Food and drink

One of the delights of travelling to different areas is sampling regional dishes, foreign cooking, and unusual food. However, a common problem that tourists face is turista, or "travellers' tum". One of the reasons travellers are prone to illness is that their **immune system** isn't always used to some of the **micro-organisms** found in unfamiliar places. Therefore, it's even more important than normal to wash hands frequently with soap and hot water when travelling to different places.

DID YOU KNOW?

A real fear of travelling is called hodophobia. And it isn't always a fear of flying. A fear of trains or of travelling in cars can also be part of this phobia. Some sufferers are afraid of strange places, open places, or of contact with strangers.

Bottle it!

One of the warnings often given to travellers going abroad is to only drink bottled water. This is because of the risk from "foreign" water organisms. The same goes for campers, as even the cleanest looking stream could be contaminated. With a little extra care, and basic medication in the first aid kit just in case, there's no reason why even the most adventurous traveller has to spend the entire trip in the bathroom!

- When you are in a place without proper **sanitation**, don't brush your teeth with tap water. Also, be careful about ice cubes in drinks, and close your mouth in the shower!

- When camping, the rule is: "boil it, cook it, peel it, or forget it!" Thorough cooking is always important.

- With meat, be extra careful and make sure it's well done on the inside. Remember, the more the food is cooked, the more likely it is that harmful bacteria have been killed.

- Do not put your fingers in your mouth, and touch food as little as possible with your hands.

- Be careful when eating that thirst-quenching melon. Bacteria can live inside melons, too, so it's better to avoid them.

- Rice contains many types of bacteria. The bacteria multiply as the rice cools. Only eat freshly cooked, hot rice.

- Take great care with shellfish – another common cause of travellers' food poisoning. But, good news, hot pizza is safe! The high heat of a pizza oven tends to kill any harmful bacteria.

Some of the food for sale on your travels might be unfamiliar!

Be prepared

Being ill far away from home or in another country is an unpleasant experience. But it is one that can be avoided with care. The usual illnesses most travellers get are not serious, but they can cause problems if medical help is far away or if you don't speak the local language. It's therefore useful to have something handy in a first aid kit to relieve headache, diarrhoea, and insect bites when travelling abroad.

It is also necessary, of course, to take any medical supplies used on a regular basis, as they may be hard to find in another country. That includes any prescription drugs, such as inhalers and **allergy** medication. It's a good idea to pack some over-the-counter allergy medication just in case. Travellers can sometimes develop allergic reactions to all kinds of things in a new environment.

Getting it Right

For journeys to the tropics, add **anti-malarial** tablets and water purification tablets to your first aid kit. After all, there could be deadly creatures in both the air and water – and they're often unseen.

• CHECKLIST •

Just in case you need to seek medical help abroad, it's wise to carry a short medical history list, with the following information on it:

- name, address, home telephone number as well as a parent's daytime telephone number;
- blood type;
- vaccinations you've had;
- doctor's name, address, and office and emergency telephone numbers;
- the name, address, telephone number, and details of any health or travel insurance;
- a list of any ongoing health problems and any current medications being taken;
- a list of allergies to medications, food, insects, and animals.

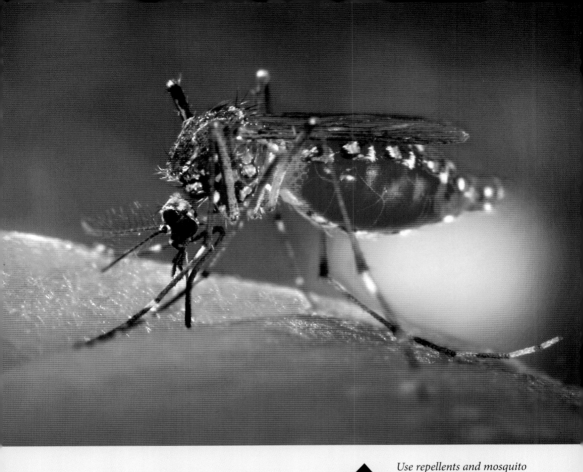

Use repellents and mosquito nets to keep blood-sucking insects at bay.

Mosquitoes

Mosquito species vary all around the world. They can be especially dangerous in the tropics where they can spread **malaria**. Mosquito bites can become very itchy and sore and can swell up if they become infected. When travelling to places where mosquitoes are common, it is important to use a mosquito repellent and to sleep under a mosquito net. Try to get a room with a large fan (the draught makes it harder for mosquitoes to fly).

Flesh wounds

Any flesh wound in the tropics is a health risk as infection can hit hard. It's sound advice to carry good plasters, especially those that seal a wound against air and water, while at the same time allowing the skin to breathe. A small amount of disinfectant and antiseptic cream in the first aid kit is useful for cleaning wounds. It's then best to get any bites, scratches, and cuts checked by a doctor, just to make sure.

extremes

Being prepared for all conditions is one of the challenges facing travellers going to many regions. Stories of travellers packing thick clothing when going to cool places, only to face a heat wave, or expecting to sunbathe on a tropical beach, only to be chilled by bitterly cold winds, are all too common. Once again, a little research and being prepared can help ensure your long-awaited holiday isn't spent suffering in unsuitable clothes.

Hidden dangers

Hiking is a great way to enjoy the wild outdoors, but care must always be taken. The weather can change quickly, so it's always best to be prepared for all weathers. Carry extra layers for the cold and waterproofs for the rain. Remember: the wind can cause **wind chill** or, in sunny conditions, even sunburn. Covering the skin is important both in cold winds and hot. In fact, hiking in very hot conditions can cause heat exhaustion.

Hiking should never be attempted once temperatures reach 37°C (100°F). Even the fittest young people can experience medical problems, even death, in such extreme conditions.

DID YOU KNOW?

Extreme heat and high altitude commonly lead to health issues among tourists. Both conditions are present at one of the most popular tourist attractions in the United States. Nearly 5 million people visit the Grand Canyon National Park in Arizona each year. It is one of the natural wonders of the world. Moving sun and shadows on the rock layers produce a breathtaking display of colours. These great cliffs were carved by the Colorado River, now snaking through the bottom of the canyon. The only way down is by hiking or riding mules down steep trails. The high altitude at the top of the Grand Canyon sometimes causes visitors to experience difficulties, particularly if they have breathing or heart problems. For most people walking at this altitude can be a struggle.

TIP

When hiking, always carry plenty of water, sun block, and a hat with a rim or peak.

Altitude sickness

At a higher altitude than you're used to, you may experience problems such as headaches, **dehydration**, and shortness of breath. Some people are affected at 1,500 metres (5,000 feet) but others aren't affected until they reach altitudes of 3,000 metres (10,000 feet) or more. Dehydration is when a person loses more fluids than they take in. If you ignore your thirst, dehydration can slow you down or even be dangerous.

Getting it Right

The best prevention for altitude sickness is gradually to increase your altitude every day to get used to it. It's always best to see a doctor before leaving home if you are planning to visit places at high altitudes.

Visitors to the Grand Canyon are warned not to hike from the top down to the river and back in one day because of the danger of dehydration and heat exhaustion.

Health tips for hiking in extreme conditions

- Do double your calorie intake and double your fun! Salty snacks and water or sports drinks should be consumed on any hike lasting longer than 30 minutes. Food is your body's fuel.

- Do drink one litre (four cups) of water or sports drink for every hour hiking. Your best defence against illness and exhaustion is to eat a large breakfast, a full lunch, a snack every time you take a drink, and a full meal at the end of the day. This is not a time to diet!

- Do know what your destination is.

- Do balance your food intake with fluid. With exertion, you lose salt and need to replace it or you may become ill.

- Do hike intelligently. You are responsible for your own safety as well as that of everyone in your party.

Getting it Wrong

- Never hike alone.
- Don't overestimate what you can do.

Hiking round the Grand Canyon can be hard work but the views are breath taking.

QUIZ

HAVING FUN

1) If going hiking, would you:
a) throw anything you can find in a rucksack and hope for the best?
b) phone up friends to join you and share the carrying?
c) map out your hiking route, with a detailed time plan, and label snacks for when they should be eaten?

2) If going to a new city, would you:
a) just turn up and see what's going on?
b) head straight for the bright lights and entertainment?
c) make a list of places to visit, in alphabetical order, with map references and telephone numbers?

3) To make sure you don't get lost on your travels, would you:
a) trust your sense of direction or just ask the way to places?
b) rely on friends to plan your route and go with the flow?
c) take three maps, a SAT-NAV, and a compass?

4) If you were to go to another country, would you:
a) forget the phrase book and just use signs and a warm smile?
b) try out every eating place you can find, letting friends choose the first few?
c) avoid eating and drinking, and scrub your hands every hour?

5) If you were to go to a sunny beach, would you:
a) slap on the sun cream and chill?
b) dive in and organise a surfing competition?
c) cover up, using a sunhat and umbrella, and cover yourself in insect repellent?

6) If you were to go to the Grand Canyon, would you:
a) sit on one of the mules and let it take you wherever it likes?
b) set off on a group hike and hope to go white-water rafting?
c) take extra oxygen to help you breathe and a huge water tank to avoid dehydration?

See page 50 to find out what kind of adventurer you are!

TROUBLESHOOTING

What's the worst thing that could happen on your travels? If you made a list of all the likely setbacks, you'd never want to go anywhere! Even though most journeys are trouble-free, you do sometimes have to consider what to do if something goes wrong.

WORST-CASE SITUATIONS

You can't prepare for all travel nightmares, but it helps if you know some of the things to do if and when they strike. Nobody likes to think about what can go wrong while they're on holiday – as the whole point of travel is to have fun. But setbacks can, and do, happen. While you can't always avoid them, you can make plans.

Lost and don't speak the language?

Whatever happens, don't panic! There's no immediate danger. Stay calm and remember your manners. People are usually quite friendly to lost strangers. Finding a police officer or a public official is the best thing to do – or head for a major tourist attraction where there should be many people to ask, including someone who can understand you! Make sure you have a good map of the area with you at all times when you set out.

Getting it Wrong

When travelling abroad, it is vital that everyone is aware of the rules, customs, and laws of the country being visited. It is no excuse to say, "I'm very sorry but I didn't know I was breaking the law." Young people, sports fans, and students are sometimes arrested for "inappropriate behaviour" in public areas, such as being noisy or appearing threatening in a large group. If people get into trouble with the police while travelling abroad, they must remain calm and polite, and contact the local embassy for help.

Ill or injured?

No one should travel abroad without travel insurance, which covers the cost of any medical treatment. Whether with an organised party, family group, or friends, each person's policy should cover the cost of transport to get to hospital, hospital fees, and getting home. All a traveller needs is the travel insurance paperwork, should an emergency arise.

TIP

When you arrive at a new hotel, always write down its name and telephone number to keep in a safe pocket incase you get lost. By keeping hold of a phrasebook, you should also be able to communicate a few well-chosen phrases if you need to, such as "help", "I'm lost", and "thank you".

A good phrasebook can be a traveller's best friend.

CRIME

Wherever young people travel, they should always be alert for criminals at work. Thieves are often on the lookout for anyone with valuables worth stealing – such as mobile phones. Theft happens everywhere, but on holiday, when you have few possessions with you, it can be even more devastating. Although no one can stop crime, most travellers can try to prevent themselves becoming victims. They do this by being constantly aware of their surroundings, personal safety, and keeping their wits about them.

Should you become a victim of crime, it is essential to report it at once to the local police. This applies wherever you happen to be travelling at the time.

Tips to reduce the risk of being a target

- Act confidently. Avoid drawing attention by "looking like a tourist". Don't stand on street corners looking at maps but walk confidently, as this will deter many criminals.

- Use a money belt, and don't carry all of your cash in one place. If you need to organise your wallet or check your money, go into a store to do so. In crowded subways, keep a wallet in a front pocket, rather than out of sight. Keep handbags closed and held in front or, better still, use secret pockets.

- Don't flaunt jewellery, cameras, souvenirs, or cash in public.

- Dress down so you don't look too flashy or draw attention to yourself.

- Be aware at all times and listen to your instincts. Tourists become victims when they're caught off guard, forget to keep a lookout, or wander away from others.

Getting it Wrong

Never open your hotel room door before identifying who is calling. Never leave your hotel alone or with someone you have just met. Never give out the number of your hotel room. Never agree to meet strangers in unknown places. Avoid quiet, badly-lit areas or the "shady" parts of town, and always stay in company. All travellers should always be aware of local customs, cultures, and attitudes to save causing offence, especially if visiting places of worship. All young travellers should keep with their party leaders or guardian at all times.

Stranger danger

Meeting new people is all part of the travelling experience and a great way to learn about new places. Sadly, the traveller has to be aware that not everybody is what, or whom, they seem.

When young people are on holiday, they go out mingling, partying, and meeting new people. That is when they are most vulnerable to being fooled. Travellers need to be careful of strangers and always be wary of what anybody offers, as there are a lot of scam artists about. Of course, that doesn't mean nobody can be trusted, but it's sometimes best to be suspicious of everyone at first.

DID YOU KNOW?

The TIA/Synovate Voice of the Traveller Survey found that although people strive to "get away from it all" on vacation, many carry a surprising amount of technology with them. Of the travellers surveyed, 86 percent took a mobile phone, 67 percent took a digital camera, and 24 percent even took a laptop. The more valuable the items you take with you, the greater the cost if they are stolen.

Be aware that although crime is rare, it does happen.

DANGERS AND SET-BACKS

No matter where you go on your travels, if nature strikes, things can get scary. Very rarely do tourists become caught up in floods, hurricanes, earthquakes, or giant **tsunamis**. There's very little anyone can do to prepare for such events, but there are a few common-sense things to do should there be sudden confusion and lack of services following a major incident.

The first thing to check when booking into a hotel is what its emergency procedure is. Hotels should also have some idea of disaster possibilities, emergency supplies, and a general plan. However, this all depends on the quality of the hotel.

If a disaster is serious, it's likely all phones will be out of action. There is likely to be much confusion at first. When possible, travellers abroad should contact their embassy. They will collect names of the **nationals** affected, inform families back home, and organise evacuation.

Preparing for the worst

So how can a traveller ever be prepared? After all, some of the most amazing parts of the world are prone to dangerous weather conditions from time to time.

Always find out what the weather forecast is at your destination for the week ahead. Typing a place name

or postcode into a weather check website (see page 52 for details) will tell you just what conditions to expect. Even so, it's still wise to keep checking, up to the time of departure, as weather forecasts can change!

TIP

Wherever you go with your friends on holiday, or when travelling, it is important to stay with them, or close by them, at all times. Keep checking on each other. If you do get separated, try to contact each other at least every hour or so. Also, arrange a meeting place in advance incase you get split up.

Despite the passing danger of a tornado in 2007, Disney World, with its thousands of visitors, remained safe.

SCARY ANIMALS

Local animal populations can prove dangerous, especially if you are camping out in the wild. Two top tourist attractions in the United States are Yosemite, in California, and Yellowstone National Park, in Wyoming. Yosemite is home to black bears, while Yellowstone is home to both black and grizzly bears. Every year a few travellers have trouble with bears.

National Park signs warn visitors about bears. Maybe bears also need signs warning them about humans?

Bearing up

Although the risk of an encounter with a bear is low, it is wise to be wary on travels through these and other parks. More often than not, the traveller is at fault and not the bear! So, just in case you come face to face with a bear on your travels, some tips might be useful:

- Make loud noises if hiking on trails.
- Don't hike after dark.
- Avoid approaching any dead animals, as bears often defend them as a source of food.
- If you encounter a bear, don't run. Bears can run faster than Olympic sprinters! If the bear is unaware of you, detour away from the bear. If the bear is aware of you but has not acted aggressively, slowly back away.
- Climbing a tree is sometimes advisable, but not very practical. All North American bears, both black and grizzly, can climb trees.
- Never feed bears. Hang food and anything with strong smells out of the reach of bears, if possible from trees far from the tent! If no trees are available, store your food in airtight or specially designed bear-proof containers.

SAFE OR SORRY?

1) If you got lost in another country, would you:
a) walk to the city centre and look for signs to the tourist information office?
b) scream and run up to the nearest passer-by?
c) climb to the top of a church tower for a better view?

2) If your money was stolen when you were far from home, would you:
a) find a police station and report the details?
b) sit in the street and cry?
c) ask everyone in the street if they took your money?

3) If a stranger knocked on your hotel door, would you:
a) use the door security chain and refuse to let them in?
b) shout at them to go away and set off an alarm?
c) welcome them in for a drink and a chat?

4) If one of your friends went missing and you were in an unfamiliar city, would you:
a) call their mobile phone and go to where you agreed to meet in an emergency?
b) run to the police in a panic, shouting "emergency!"?
c) carry on as normal and hope they show up?

5) If a tornado was forecast to hit your holiday resort, would you:
a) ask advice at the hotel and stay calm?
b) scream to everyone to join you lying face-down in a ditch?
c) go swimming to get out of the way?

See page 50 to find out how safe a traveller you are!

Think Green

No book about travel can ignore the effect tourism is having on our planet. People moving from one place to another use a lot of energy and that means there is always a cost to the environment. Much of the energy we use for transport leaves pollution behind.

CARBON FOOTPRINT

Many places are trying to reduce the amount of carbon dioxide they release into the atmosphere. So travellers need to think about the impact they might be making with their "carbon footprint". This is the total amount of carbon dioxide we each produce that has an impact on the environment.

Getting it Right

- Do you really need to take that plane? Could you get to your destination using more eco-friendly ways of travel? How about exploring areas closer to home?

- Before booking a holiday with a tour operator, travellers should ask whether the company has a "green policy". Cleaner travel sometimes costs more, so if people are serious about saving the planet, they should be prepared to pay a little extra.

- When hiking, always stay on marked trails and keep a distance from any animals. Put rubbish in marked bins or take it home. Light campfires only in designated areas, well away from dry grass and trees, making sure the ashes are cold before moving on.

- When diving in the sea, do not touch coral or stir up sediment, as these actions can damage a reef's fragile ecosystem.

- Buy local products whenever possible, instead of goods flown or shipped in from overseas. This will support local people and their economy.

Nearly one billion tourists criss-cross the globe every year. Therefore it is more important than ever for travellers to respect the Earth that they want to explore. So when visiting the world's beautiful places, keep this old saying in mind:

> *"Take nothing but photographs, leave nothing but footprints, kill nothing but time."*
> *Unknown*

Some airlines are soon hoping to use bio-fuel, which is far cleaner for the environment.

Bon voyage!

By travelling we can learn so much more about the world, others, and ourselves. Travelling should help us all to respect others and become more sensitive to other people's customs, beliefs, and lifestyles. Every traveller has a responsibility to respect the landscape, people, and wildlife they visit, as well as the wider environment. Particularly with growing fears that global warming may damage forever the very places we long to visit.

There are sometimes risks, but with care, the whole experience of travelling can be amazing. We all have a part to play – so enjoy thoughtful travel!

 RESULTS

GETTING THERE
For page 19

If you mostly answered:

a) You prefer your own company and are quite independent. You travel to get away from the rat-race.

b) You want a holiday on the cheap and save as much money as you can.

c) You like a bit of luxury, good company, and you don't mind what it costs.

SAFE OR SORRY?
For page 47

If you mostly answered:

a) You remain calm and sensible in a crisis, making you a good travelling companion.

b) You panic easily and do not cope well in a crisis.

c) You haven't taken this book, or its advice, seriously.

HAVING FUN
For page 39

If you mostly answered:

a) You're so laid-back that you don't bother with much preparation — so anything could happen!

b) You're lively and want to enjoy an active holiday with lots of friends.

c) You take planning seriously but may be a little overcautious at times!

(20) THINGS TO REMEMBER

1 The number-one rule when packing is "if in doubt, leave it out" to avoid carrying too much.

2 A good online currency converter can show the value of most world currencies when you travel abroad.

3 *Never* hitchhike on your travels, even in a group.

4 Ginger or peppermint may help if you suffer from seasickness or general travel sickness.

5 When flying, check flight times and possible delays online before leaving for the airport.

6 When making a hotel booking by phone or online, keep a record of a confirmation number, the name of the person who took the reservation, and the quoted cost. Keep this in case there is a problem on arrival.

7 For young people needing cheap, reliable accommodation for just a night or two, try an approved youth hostel.

8 When looking for a spot to pitch a tent, avoid windy hilltops and the bottom of hills, where you're at risk of being blown away or flooded.

9 Leave a copy of your travel plans with someone back home so, if you lose anything, help is an email or phone call away.

10 Wherever you are, keep with friends/leaders, don't wander off alone, and always have a mobile phone handy.

11 Don't drink tap water abroad, or brush your teeth with it – just in case.

12 Worried about food poisoning and not sure what to eat? Try piping hot pizza – usually safe from bacteria!

13 Always take and use mosquito repellent and sleep under a mosquito net in the tropics.

14 Salty snacks and water or sports drinks should be consumed on any hike lasting longer than 30 minutes.

15 Keep a copy of your hotel's name and phone number on you at all times, in case you get lost.

16 Use a money belt, and don't carry all your cash at once.

17 Avoid being the victim of crime by not looking too flashy or like a typical tourist.

18 When hiking, always stay on marked trails and keep a distance from animals. In bear country, be loud so they know to keep away.

19 Buying local products on your travels supports the local economy and is all part of "green travel".

20 Keep in touch with the folks back home – either by regular emails or texts.

Further Information

Websites

http://www.who.int/ith/en/
Find out what you need to know about vaccinations before you go!

http://www.greyhound.com/home/
Get timetable and route information for travelling in the U.S. and Canada.

http://nationalexpress.com/
Information on travelling in the UK by both bus and train.

http://eurolines.com
See how to travel by bus to over 500 places in Europe.

http://www.hihostels.com/
Make the most of your hostel experience by knowing where to go.

http://www.abc-of-hiking.com/
Information about everything and anything related to hiking and camping.

http://www.hostels.com/
This is a mega-database of more than 10,000 hostels to check out.

http://www.travel-library.com/
Looking for accommodation? Find details for hotels and vacation rentals here.

http://www.lonelyplanet.com/
Travel advice and information for just about every place on the planet.

http://www.dk.com/
Illustrated travel guides, complete with maps of the best sights to visit.

http://www.roughguides.com/
Travel guides packed full of "off the beaten track" information for the more serious traveller.

http://weather.yahoo.com/
Know before you go what's happening with the weather.

http://www.travelpost.com/articles/safe-travel-tips.aspx
A run down of travel tips to keep you safe on your travels.

http://realtravel.com/
Get advice from other travellers.

http://travel.state.gov/
U.S. Department of State Updates of international situations which may pose a problem for your travels.

http://www.timeout.com
Gain an insight of cultural goings on in many of the world's large cities, including museum, music, art and cinema listings, and restaurant and hotel reviews.

BOOKS/GUIDES

Fodor's 1,001 Smart Travel Tips (Fodor's, 2008).

Make the Most of Your Time on Earth: a Rough Guide to the World, 1,000 Ultimate Travel Experiences (Rough Guides, 2007).

The Smart Traveller's Passport: 399 Tips from Seasoned Travellers, Erik Torkells (Quirk Books, 2007).

Where to Go When, Craig Doyle (Dorling Kindersley, 2007).

GLOSSARY

acupressure method of applying pressure on specific points of the body to control pain and sickness

allergy abnormal reaction (like sneezing, itching, or rashes) to substances and situations

anti-malarial serving to prevent, control, or cure malaria

dehydration loss of water or body fluids

dormitory room for sleeping, especially for several people

ecosystem system made up of living things interacting with their environment

eco-friendly ecologically acceptable; not harmful or threatening to the environment

embassy office of an ambassador and staff representing a country overseas

etiquette the rules governing the proper way to behave

exchange rate rate at which one currency may be converted into another

homesick longing for home and family while away from them

hurricane type of storm featuring violent winds, rain, thunder, and lightning

immune system system that protects the body from foreign substances and disease

jaywalking walking across a street outside of marked crossings or against a signal light

long-haul travelling for eight or more hours

malaria disease passed by the bite of mosquitoes, and marked by attacks of chills and fever

micro-organisms microscopic life or less than microscopic size (such as bacteria)

nationals people who are under the protection of a nation

phobia unreasonable and lasting fear of something

prestigious important in the eyes of many people

sanitation sewage systems and water treatment to promote hygiene and prevent disease

tandem bicycle for two riders

tariff list of rates or charges of a business or service

tornado destructive, whirling wind, with a funnel-shaped cloud that moves across the land

tsunami giant ocean wave caused by an earthquake at sea

vaccinations vaccines, usually by injection, that protect against disease

visa document that may be required for someone to enter another country or to stay there for a long period

wind chill temperature felt on exposed skin due to wind speed – colder than the air temperature

YHA Youth Hostel Association

Index

A

accommodation 20–25
acupressure 14
air travel 16–18, 48–49
airsickness 16
allergies 34
altitude sickness 36–37
animals 46
anti-malarial tablets 34
ATMs 11

B

B & B (bed and breakfast) 21
bags 8, 9
bears 46
bicycles 12
boats 14
booking accommodation 20
bus travel 13, 30

C

camping 24–25, 32, 33
car travel 13
carbon footprint 48
carsickness 13
cities 26–31
clothes 28, 36
costs, in cities 26
crime 29, 42, 43
cruise ships 14
currency exchange 11
customs inspections 10

D

dehydration 18, 37, 38
documents 10
dormitories 22
dress codes 28
drugs, prescription 34

E

eco-friendly 48
ecosystems 48
emails 7
embassies 10, 40, 44
emergencies 44
equipment, camping 24
etiquette 10, 40
exchange rate 11

F

fear of travelling 32
first aid kit 9, 34
flesh wounds 35
flying 16–18, 48–49
food and drink 32–33, 38, 46
food poisoning 32, 33

G

GPS (Global Positioning Satellite) systems 30
Grand Canyon 36–38
guesthouses 21

H

health care 32–38, 41
heat exhaustion 36
hiking 24, 36, 38, 46, 48
hitchhiking 13
homesickness 7
hostels 21, 22–23
hotels 20, 21, 41, 42, 44
hurricanes 6, 44
hygiene 32

I

illness 34, 41
immune system 32
inoculations 11
insurance 41
Internet 7, 28

J

jaywalking 28

L

languages 10, 40, 41
laws 28, 40
loneliness 7
long-haul travel 5
lost, getting 40
luggage 8–9, 16, 18

M

malaria 34
maps 40
medication 34
metro 30
micro-organisms 32
mobile phones 29, 42, 43
money 11, 42
mosquitoes 35
motels 21

N

nationals 44
New York 26–27

P

packing 8–9
passports 10, 29
phobias 32
phones 29, 42, 43
phrasebooks 41
pickpockets 29, 42, 43
planning 6–7, 28, 36
police 40, 41
prestigious 14
problems 40–47
public transport 30

R

rail travel 14–15, 30
research 6, 28
road travel 12–13
rucksacks 8
"rules of the road" 13, 22, 34

S

safety 13, 30, 40–47
sanitation 33
satellite navigation devices (SAT-NAVs) 30–31
sea travel 14
seasickness 14
self-catering accommodation 21
star system, hotels 20
stranger danger 43
street codes 28
subways 30

T

tandems 12
tariffs 20
theft 29, 42, 43
tornadoes 44
traffic jams 12
trains 14–15, 30
travel 12–19
traveller's cheques 11
"travellers' tum" 32
troubleshooting 40–47
tsunamis 44

U

underground trains 30

V

vaccinations 11
visas 10

W

walking 24, 36, 38, 46, 48
water 32, 33
weather 6, 36, 44
wind chill 36
wounds 35

Y

YHA (Youth Hostel Association) 22–23